Fifty Things
You Must Never Do

If You Are a
Woman over Fifty

Maria Larson Manske

Larson Manske

Introduction

When milestones occur in people's lives often they seek the solace of the self-help section in the bookstore or library. About to have a baby? Plenty of books on that subject. How about getting married? There is an entire industry on that as well. When you reach an age where career choices dwindle, wrinkles are on the rise, and your friends no longer care to listen to Led Zeppelin until two o'clock in the morning, you might also think you need a little guidance, if not a straight-up pep talk. This little book is not about what you can do to make turning fifty a fun and fabulous time. It's about how to save yourself from receiving unwanted stares, and generally living with a bumbling sense of cluelessness while acting like you know what's going down. How do I know this? Because I've learned the hard way. Guilty of many of the fifty "don'ts" that follow here, I can attest to their embarrassment factor. Why add to the stress of hot flashes, unsuccessful (and sadly, ongoing) attempts to defy gravity, and the increasing inability to remember anything? We are over fifty now. We should know better, right? Once we get these crimes out of the way we can start a clean slate. My next book will be about the fifty fun and fabulous things you must do once turning fifty. Stay tuned!

Maria Larson Manske
September 2012

An archaeologist is the best husband a woman can have. The older she gets the more interested he is in her. —Agatha Christie

Wrinkles should merely indicate where smiles have been. —Mark Twain

Forty is the old age of youth, fifty is the youth of old age. —Hosea Ballou

Youth is the gift of nature, but age is a work of art.

—Stanislaw Lec

To my late Aunt Dorothy, who was loved by all who knew her, and could wear green eye shadow unlike any other woman. Most of all, this book is for my late mother, who was down to earth and never afraid to laugh at herself.

ONE

Lie about your age.

Face the facts in the mirror. You think people don't see what you see? In school I was never very good at math only because other activities such as reading, writing, and observing all the other more interesting things around me took my attention instead, like the way the dust settled after the teacher erased the blackboard, how Heidi's pure white knee highs always seemed to stay up on her legs, and the curious names given to Crayola crayons. There is one basic thing about numbers that I have not forgotten, however: I have not lost count of my age. Not that I have employed any of these measures, but I believe that even if you run for two hours a day, do yoga for another two, are able to afford, shop for and cook macrobiotic meals, and have time to meditate and thereby clearing the detritus of day-to-day Western living from your slate, you cannot mess with your body's odometer.

If you do choose to lie about your age, then be prepared to lie about a bunch of other stuff as well. You will need a database to keep track of it all. Good luck!

TWO

Think that you are about to live your "best life."

It's time to face it. Your early thirties were a blast and there is no turning back. Moreover, the last time I checked, humans have but *one* life, no? The use of the word "best" implies there are others, such as good, better, etc. We're not cats and get to pick, say, number five or seven as our "best life." Am I right about this?

THREE

If divorced or looking for extramarital escapades you believe that it's not too late to be a Cougar.

When a recently "freed-up" woman aged around fifty walks into a bar or crashes your party, the kind who feels as though for decades she has been caged against her will and now—only now—can she really be herself, you will notice her like some escapee spotlighted in a prison yard. Inevitably her skirt is too tight or too short, make-up all wrong, and handbag is as big as her ass or studded with diamante or both. If you think you will find your next best life searching for meaning and looking this way, you are wrong.

FOUR

Think that wearing white skirts or pants before May 31st is bunk.

Wearing white at any time of the year is fine, as long as you are a surgeon, member of a religious order, line cook, or an anorexic bride. The rest of us, especially women over fifty, should think hard about our choices.

FIVE

Play Abba and Bread after too many drinks at an otherwise agreeable dinner with friends at home.

As a teen you may have spent late July evenings in your bedroom dancing around your crappy little orange Sears stereo, or in Brian's pick-up truck with the AM radio blasting at a keg party listening to tunes. Fast forward to a decent meal in the new millennium with your current adult friends (who probably listened to the same music but not with the same sentimentality or photographic memory of liner notes) and you decide to haul out the memories in haphazard stacks of cassettes and CDs. Your guests look on half smiling, looking at their watches as you sing bad harmony to "Fernando." There are these things now called mp3 players with headphones. And you get to create playlists with them and everything. Do that, and do it often. But keep the playlists to yourself.

SIX

Keep shoes from 1991 you never wore then, either.

We all have them. I have a pair of rust suede slip-ons I never wore, but I swear to God they are not going to the DAV or Goodwill. So, they take up room in my dusty shoe bag under my bed. One more thing my daughter has to deal with after I'm gone.

SEVEN

Say things like "like" "awesome" and "dude" in an effort to effectively communicate with teen offspring.

Who am I to knock down anyone's effort to get in good with the kids? Be honest and tell them how you feel, while taking into account their perspective and stage in life. But this doesn't mean you must adopt a vocabulary that makes you sound like an imbecile.

EIGHT

If your toes are less than perfect, wear frosty black or neon pink nail polish your daughter "left behind."

Feet are weird. We all know this. Yet for some women, hardworking toes are treated as though they must look like jewels. The popularity of pedicures proves this. Yet why, when asked, "Pick a color!" or looking in your daughter's vanity drawer do many women over fifty insist on falling in love with the wrong color? Why draw attention to toes that are beginning to take on the appearance of ginger root? Anyone heard of pale pink? Less is more here, for sure.

NINE

At every monthly book club meeting spend half the night talking about the time you had sex with someone other than a relatively privileged American guy.

Here we go again. You really loved Giovanni. He was amazing. That one month you spent on the "continent." We've heard it, sister. A million times. Do you want to keep your friends? The ones who have not had a beefy Italian whisper nonsensical nothings in their ears? Well then keep this little chapter to yourself.

TEN

Show any hint of thong.

Sure, if you must. But how any fifty year-old ass looks good in a thong is beyond me and everyone else (except desperate lonely truckers.)

ELEVEN

Think that going to Target or Wal-Mart braless in a loose t-shirt while wearing your pajama bottoms and flip flops is OK because you are dressing like and therefore bonding with your daughter.

If you are truly bonding your daughter, you would be setting an example of how to dress when out in public.

TWELVE

Burger King, McDonald's, Wendy's, Hardees, Sonic, Taco Bell, Arby's or Zantigo for breakfast, lunch, dinner, fourth meal, or any other drive-thru moment.

When was fast food ever a good idea? Possibly when you were seven-years old and your dad took you to McDonald's after a day at the beach. In high school when you cruised around the neighborhood in Dave's jacked up Malibu, and ended up in the parking lot of Burger King flicking fries at each other as a juvenile form of foreplay. Well, those romantic days are gone. And so are the days of fast food if you want to live beyond fifty-five.

THIRTEEN

Start up a cupcake shop and expect to have fun 24/7.

This is often a time when people say to themselves: "What have I done with my life, exactly? I've always wanted to (fill in the blank)." Thanks to a host of food reality TV shows and cupcake shops that seem to be springing up on every gentrified corner of any city you care to explore, many women believe that they can be cupcake queens! Make cute cupcakes in all kinds of crazy colors and flavor combinations and sell them! Well, the reality is that you will be smothered in business bureaucracy: tax burdens, landlord nightmares, Chamber politics, the drama of hiring, keeping and firing staff, and the price of vegetable shortening. Instead of starting a small business you know nothing about, just go work in one of these places and get it out of your system. Keep your day job, and your dignity.

FOURTEEN

Willingly put yourself amongst a much younger sweaty crowd at an outdoor music festival wearing a wonky white tennis visor, halter top (showing overly-sunned shoulders) while drinking Bud Light.

When Woodstock happened you were what, in the 4th grade? Yes, you missed out, but time to get over it. Since then there have been plenty of outdoor festival opportunities to make up for it. If you have not found them by now it's time to move on.

FIFTEEN

In bed by nine o'clock with a heating pad when you're not even sick.

Treat yourself like an old lady and see what happens.

SIXTEEN

Complain at length to your twenty-two year-old waitress about the food that has totally ruined your evening.

I know the feeling. After working your ass off all week, you finally allow yourself to indulge at a good restaurant with a friend (or lover or spouse) yet, the food, atmosphere, table setting—whatever—disappoints. You looked forward to this. You are feeling a bit hot and menopausy and you want your best life, so you take it out on the skinny, beautiful girl who speeds past you all night balancing cocktails and entrees on her sinewy arms. One, you are simply envious of her. Bad deal. Two, this meal at this particular restaurant is not a barometer of some kind of impending doom in your life, so please: chill.

SEVENTEEN

At the produce section in the grocery store, rip the husks off corn and toss them into the bin until you find the perfect ears.

This is especially bad if while you are decimating perfectly good produce that no other customer will now touch, you are talking on your cell phone to your son who from the sounds of it, despite your worn advice, simply cannot get his act together.

EIGHTEEN

Attend your high school reunion thinking you are a fox.

Worse yet, attempt an impossible diet for three months before the event which will be held at some shitty Holiday Inn overflowing with fat bald guys you wouldn't want to recognize anyway. And if you're there to find that one girl in the basketball team on which you secretly had a forbidden crush, do you honestly think she would be at this reunion to get more harassment for being a "lesbo" from people who are now fat bald guys, or people like you who are trying to bleach blonde their way back into a lost forever youth?

NINETEEN

Continually repeat yourself at every work happy hour, as though you are saying for the first time, that your job sucks and in a parallel universe you are really Elizabeth Gilbert or Jane Goodall.

So why don't you go and quit your job and do Europe and Indonesia? Or go live in Africa and study monkeys. No one, and I mean no one, is stopping you.

TWENTY

For regular meal planning actually *use* the Betty Crocker cookbook your mom gave you, instead of simply letting it provide retro décor.

Even if all you can do to improve on this situation is to buy a Sandra Lee cookbook, then do it. Now.

TWENTY-ONE

For the first time in your life start a daily running routine around your neighborhood (or anyone else's) while wearing expensive fitness gear.

I am not one to say it's never too late. But in this case, it is. Thin running shorts and bright green athletic bras look good on people who run. That's what they're made for. Not for you and me.

TWENTY-TWO

Botox.

In Western society generally women stress about age and laugh lines (which only makes them worse). In many other cultures around the world, these natural things are symbols of experience and often generate respect. If Botox is your drug of choice to help you believe you're much younger than you are, for most us unfortunate onlookers, all you do is simply look really weird.

TWENTY-THREE

Still think that fad diets work.

It's been said that the definition of insanity is doing the same thing over and over and expecting different results each time.

TWENTY-FOUR

With the curiosity of a cat, look up and connect with former lovers on Facebook. .

What, exactly, do you hope to gain from this? Are you going to run off and meet this person in some city or Godforsaken tavern where neither your current lover nor mate can find you? And then what? They are likely to be as older as you are older yet certainly none the wiser. Keep him or her in the past where they belong. Remember: it ended for a reason.

TWENTY-FIVE

Sun beds.

A beef jerky patina on what are already wrinkly knees and elbows is a desired look?

TWENTY-SIX

Clip coupons.

So you saved a dollar! Woo hoo! On junk you don't even need. Save this sad activity for when you're in the assisted living home and you actually need something to get all excited about.

TWENTY-SEVEN

Wear any garment emblazoned with kittens, puppies, or Mary Englebreit illustrations.

I debated over and over about including this one here. Pretty obvious, right? But still, in the Midwest at least, I see this heinous style on women younger than me. The only exception is if you're a Grandma already (and God Bless You if you are). I have nothing against Mary Englebreit, either. But please, save her work for a greeting card to your aunt.

TWENTY-EIGHT

Wear beige or black sandals with thick adjustable Velcro straps.

I know you are all getting sick of feet here and for that I apologize. However, unless you've been wearing Dr. Scholl's your entire life up to this point, you are dealing with support issues. If you plan to keep walking, sensible shoes are indeed in your future. I don't mean you now must order all your footwear from the back of *Parade* magazine. And there are better alternatives to Velcro (well, only as far as feet are concerned, of course). Just be prepared to shell out a couple hundred for decent European footwear.

TWENTY-NINE

Believe that how much weight you carry determines your place and value in life.

Try spending even 50% of the time you think about your weight and perceived inadequacies instead on what makes you happy and gives you fulfillment. And I am not talking about hamburgers.

THIRTY

Wear retro rock t-shirts sold in the Boys Department.

This one is really hard to resist. Rush's *2112*? Led Zeppelin's *Houses of the Holy*? OK, maybe not Rush because I never really liked them nor understood anyone who did, but I am still all over Jimmy Page, gray hair and all. I'm just not sure I need to advertise that on my fifty year-old boobs.

THIRTY-ONE

Give the finger to anyone.

To witness a mature woman giving the finger, particularly while driving, is really unsettling even if you're not the guilty recipient. It doesn't look good on anybody, especially you.

THIRTY-TWO

Proudly display faded black-n-blue tats on any part of your body.

Were you one of those late boomers/early GenXers who caught the tattoo fever as way to finally, somehow, show the world how unique you really are? How this ends up is that your "Native American inspired" design running up your arm will inadvertently take center stage as you talk with your child's eighth grade teacher about her crappy math scores. There are tops with sleeves. Save the ones without them for your college reunions and the Fringe Fest.

THIRTY-THREE

Expect perfect highlights from a $10 box from Walgreens.

I am all for DIY and being thrifty, but be aware that if you insist on being blond but would rather avoid the brassy sheen of an old doorknob, please, check in at your nearest hairdresser. Even Cost Cutters will bring it better than the drugstore box.

THIRTY-FOUR

Spend $100 on a jar of skin cream from anywhere.

I recall reading a skincare article in some magazine in the '70s where a chemist from one of the large high-end cosmetic firms quoted that a woman could simply use Ponds or Vaseline and still have beautiful skin. (I am sure the company's PR people went and killed him shortly after the magazine hit the stands). Just to be clear, I am not a dermatological chemist from the '70s, but I do believe that the key to good skin is a result of the mixture of favorable genes, how much water you drink, how much sleep you get, amount of sun protection you are willing to slather on, and a solid skin care regimen. There are so many products out there right now, but the best ones tend to have few if any petrochemical or animal-derived ingredients. Along with staying away from KFC, vodka and Little Debbies (especially as a meal) I also think that minimal stress, a decent washcloth, and

41

optimum sex has a great deal to do with the appearance of skin. If you're happy, and you have a fairly good idea of what it means to eat decently and be clean, inevitably it will show in the body's biggest organ.

THIRTY-FIVE

Venture backstage at some casino concert to meet your teenage idol.

You are one of a million and he is only being nice so you can add a blurry cell phone photo to your already desperate Facebook page.

THIRTY-SIX

Wear clothes from the Juniors Department.

Yeah, it's a cute top. But buy it for your daughter or niece and spare us.

THIRTY-SEVEN

Get all excited about staying at a Victorian bed and breakfast inn.

Didn't people stop doing this in the '90s? I've nothing against Victorian architecture or aesthetics, nor is my cynicism beyond hope in that I need to complain about well-intentioned hospitality. But why must the experience inevitably include weird smells in the hallways, non-existent sound-proofing, bad "French" toast overloaded with Country Crock margarine, all served up with complete silence and ungainly stares from fellow guests, and the distracting hairstyle of the owner as she meddles and hovers throughout the "intimate dining area"?

THIRTY-EIGHT

Forward email chain letters festooned with puppies and sparkly clip art.

One, it shows that you are superstitious, if not sentimental beyond belief. Not that that's a bad thing, but there are better ways to show it. Two, that first generation clip art is really, really annoying.

THIRTY-NINE

Smoke.

You know that hacking cough that comes out of your throat every three minutes? No one says anything to you because they think it might be unkind. But really, it's disturbing. Not only because of the sound, but because we feel for your lungs and the stress they are dealing with. The smoke puffs that gather above your head as you exhale do not do much for your image, either. I am not one to criticize anyone's ability to wrangle with the force of addiction, but there are ways to deal with the cigarette thing. Try a patch. No one has to see it and it might give your lungs (and us) a break.

FORTY

Fall for AARP's membership drive.

Even before I turned fifty they were on my ass to
sign up. F&*k you!

FORTY-ONE

Buy an RV twice the size of Willie Nelson's tour bus.

Imagine that you are a mellow family with a couple of tents in a heretofore quiet, well kept, particularly beautiful campground. It's dusk and the marshmallows are toasting over the fire, mosquitoes biting on cue. Then, the Happy Trails Blazer MEGA 3000 pulls up and parks in the campsite next to you. It has been on the road for 10 hours and needs to regenerate. So, the not unquiet generator goes on and stays on for the next 4 hours while you and your quiet family are trying to get some more quiet in this otherwise quiet campground. But you can't because of the voracious appetite of the Happy Trails Blazer MEGA 3000 that has to generate power enough to flush the mini-toilet, run the water, bright the lights, and force the air conditioning for the "campers" within who have ruined your night.

Do you want to be one of these over-fifty couples who ruins everyone else's night? Think about it.

FORTY-TWO

Refuse to make peace with your mother.

I mean, you are now more like her than ever so you might as well get on with it and quit the drama. Plus, she really does love you. Even if to you she has a really screwed up way of showing it.

FORTY-THREE

Keep buying self-help books.

What makes you think one more will do the trick?

FORTY-FOUR

Get a short haircut you think is liberating yet makes you look like Sergeant Carter from *Gomer Pyle*.

We have all seen them. Women with loose, mostly always colorful clothing, sensible shoes, "What if the Hokey Pokey is What it's All About" bumper sticker and the buzz-cut of an Apollo astronaut. I am all for short hair on women—and mostly these are the sort of "what the hell" kind of women for whom I've nothing but admiration. However, unless you are bravely dealing with illness, you are a prison guard, or you are able to pull off the look Phranc achieved in the mid '80s, you should protest loudly when your hairdresser pulls out the electric clippers.

FORTY-FIVE

Continue to hold on to those low cut Levi's you haven't worn since 2004.

They didn't really fit you then, either. Your body is not returning to its former state. Even with a vegan diet and the neurotic, self-obsessed lifestyle of a Hollywood fitness trainer.

FORTY-SIX

Enter reality television show contests.

If you happen to be one of thousands that get far enough to even be a candidate for the cutting room floor, one day that footage will not look good—and your children will hate you forever.

FORTY-SEVEN

Wear your hair long parted down the middle and never get a trim.

You have not been in 1975 since 1975. (See, this is where my math, once again, comes in handy). Unless you fancy Sasquatch as a mate, get thee to a hairdresser, now.

FORTY-EIGHT

Spend more than a minute or two in front of a well-lit magnifying mirror.

I love luxury hotels. Well, I love the idea of them, because my actual experience staying in them is next to nil. But the few I've been in have all had those round magnifying mirrors coming from the marble tiled walls in the bathroom. You wipe the steam from them after your shower and look at your clean, ruddy face. Then, like wearing glasses for the first time after they are well overdue, you start to see what it's really all about. Hair. Discoloration. Random undulations. Crevices. Pores that would make an orange envious. Next time you're at The Drake or The Ritz or some European digs with 500% mark up, bypass that puppy when exiting the shower. Leave the wonders of magnification and detail to your aesthetician. She went to school and got a *license* to deal with such things. And if you don't have one, go find her, now. (And do not—do not—forget to tip her well).

FORTY-NINE

Wear cheap pants with a gathered elastic waistband.

These heinous garments should be found in your wardrobe only when you just don't care anymore. At fifty, you should still care.

FIFTY

Keep apologizing for not being able to remember anything anymore.

Along with caving in to comfy elastic waistbands, shoes with thick Velcro straps, and constantly wearing your reading glasses half down your face— this admittance of failing memory will age you immediately. When masochistically self-induced or cruelly prompted to recall what you cannot, simply say "Never mind - wouldn't want to bore you with that one...way to much detail." And watch how fast everyone is glad that the subject has automatically changed anyway. All good.

Author's Note

Do you agree or completely disagree with my blathering here? Would you like to add a few suggestions of your own? I want to hear from you! Visit my blog:

50somethinghipster.wordpress.com

Printed in Great Britain
by Amazon.co.uk, Ltd.,
Marston Gate.